The ABCs of Central Park

An Alphabet Guidebook

E 75

C 75

*Dedicated to my wife Inés and children Tamara, Sarah and Daniel
and to my grandchildren Dylan, Emily and Tyler
in appreciation for all they have taught and will teach me.*

The ABCs of Central Park
An Alphabet Guidebook

A-Z & 0-10
in photographs
by G. Augustine Lynas

C65

LYNAS PRESS
NEW YORK CITY

E106

Key to locating Central Park sites.
Look at the corner of each photograph.

W= West Side, E= East Side,
Numbers = Nearest Street

Example: C69-72 means near the Center of
the park, between 69th & 72nd Streets.

FIRST EDITION

Library of Congress Control Number: 2005938104
Library of Congress-in-Publication data is available upon request.
Printed and bound in Canada by Friesens.

ISBN No. 0-9772877-0-X
06 07 08 09   10 9 8 7 6 5 4 3 2 1

On the front cover: The Alice in Wonderland Statue by Spanish sculptor José de Creeft E75.
On the dedication page: Rustic Bench in the Ramble C75.
On the previous page: The Carousel C65.
On this page: Untermeyer Fountain by German sculptor Walter Schott (Conservatory Garden) E106.

ALPHA-BRANCHES

Letters and numbers can inspire creativity all by themselves. They become a key to all learning and open doors to many worlds. Central Park, which helps me to find peace and quiet in a huge metropolis, inspired this special alphabet discovered in the tree branches of the park. This book, printed on the product of trees, is also dedicated to the joy of learning, to the love of letters and words, and to the love of our beautiful park.

A note to readers: Having taught many children to read, and having been an educator for decades, I have avoided using "baby words" to illustrate the alphabet and numbers. Many children will not be able to say most of the bigger words at first, so please be patient and stick with it. Children have amazing capacities to absorb complex information.   GL

LETTERS

Aa

**is for Alice
in Wonderland
and angel and arch.**

Bb

is for big building, the beautiful Bow Bridge, boats, and baseball.

C80-86

C73

Cc

is for
castle
and
colorful
carousel.

C79

C65

Dd

is for dog.

Ee

is for egret.

Ff

is for firetruck number forty-four,
and a few firefighters
having lunch in the park.

Gg

is for the green grass of the Great Lawn on a gorgeous day.

Hh

is for horses and hansom carriages.

Li is for ice on the lake.

W73

C95

W81

Jj

is for just one jogger and just one juggler.

Kk

is for kite and for kiosk.

E72

C80-86

L l

is for lawn bowling and lying lazily on a rock.

Mm
is for Metropolitan Museum of Art.

E 80-84

Nn

is for North Meadow
and nighttime.

See p.47

Oo

is for
Olmsted,
obelisk,
and outing.

C 81

Pp

is for playground, path, pink petals, and painter.

Qq is for quiet.

E72

Rr

is for reservoir,
runners in a race and
red leaves on a tree.

W88

W81

C81

Ss

is for Sheep Meadow, and splashing in the sprinklers in summer.

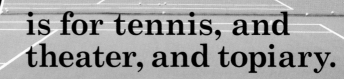

Tt

is for tennis, and theater, and topiary.

C 80

W 94-96

W 66

Uu

is for underpass,
and upside down.

E77-78

C 66-67

Vv

is for volleyball and Vaux.

See p.47

Ww

is for waterfall.

W102

X is for x-ing swords.

Xx

Yy

is for youngsters on swings,
and yellow flowers.

W85-86

Zz

is for zoo, and one for kids too.

NUMBER-LIMBS

O people on the Great Lawn after a heavy rain, or in the Sheep Meadow after a heavy snow.

W 66-69

C 80-86

1

fountain, 1 flag, and 1 wheel on a unicycle

C72

2 geese and
2 people

3 big, brown, bronze bears, and a baby boy

4 big balloons
in 4 bright
colors

5

boys playing basketball
and 1 boy watching

6
white sailboats

7 red and yellow tulips and 7 turtles on a log

8 juggling clubs

9 New Yorkers learning to fish

10 columns on the boathouse

A note to older readers:

y making this book, some trees were cut down to make the paper. Those trees should be replaced as soon as possible. We also used some chemicals, solvents, inks, machines, glue, oil, water, detergents, electricity and much more. We made noise, we transported raw materials and eventually, the finished books. But this book is not really finished. Someday it will be recycled into the natural environment. During its life as a book, I hope it will inspire its readers to respect the beautiful park it represents and, by extension, the natural world. I hope that the children who learn from this book will eventually learn of the many hidden costs in making it.

The author / photographer has avoided making a CD version of this book so that young children learning the alphabet *will not be sitting at a computer* but *will be in close, human contact* with a caring parent, a sibling, relative, friend, teacher, or care-giver who can answer their questions.

G. Augustine Lynas is a New York City artist best known as a sand sculptor. He started his professional career as a graphic designer and art director specializing in children's books. For twenty years, he taught courses in Communication Arts at Pratt Institute in Brooklyn, NY. He is also the author, photographer, book designer (and sculptor) for his book *Sandsong* (St. Martin's Press). His portfolio can be seen on his web site Sandsong.com. Mr. Lynas is married and has three grown children and three grandchildren. He goes into Central Park almost every day to rejuvenate his spirit and to enjoy its beauty and many wonders.

E86

The font used in this book is Century Schoolbook.

The Co-designers of Central Park

Frederick Law Olmsted (1822-1903) was born in Hartford, CT, the son of a successful dry-goods merchant. A restless and troubled spirit, he was a gentleman farmer in Connecticut and Staten Island, NY, for a time, wrote books about his travels in England and the South, and developed a keen love of nature. He strongly believed in the healing powers of open spaces. By chance, Olmsted learned of the plan to create a central park in New York City through a friend who was one of the commissioners. He applied, and was appointed superintendent, initially responsible for the land-clearing operation under Chief Engineer Viele.

Calvert Vaux, who had only met Olmsted one time but knew of his reputation and his similar views, suggested that they work together on a design. Their "Greensward" plan took six months of intense work to evolve and won the $2000 first prize against thirty-two other contestants. A lifelong friendship was born and a productive professional collaboration blossomed. The 20-year construction of the park provided badly needed work for roughly a thousand European immigrants.

In 1865, Vaux was asked to work on the design of Prospect Park in Brooklyn. He asked Olmsted to work on it with him and they formed the partnership Olmsted, Vaux and Company. As a team, they designed one of the first suburbs of Chicago, IL, and major parks in Buffalo, NY, among others. The partnership dissolved in 1872 and Vaux went on to pursue more architectural commissions.

Olmsted continued to leave his mark across the country by designing Riverside and Morningside Parks in NYC, the grounds of the U.S. Capitol, and parks in Boston, Montreal, Philadelphia, Baltimore, San Francisco, and other cities. In 2003, Central Park celebrated its 150th anniversary.

Calvert Vaux (1824-1895) was a British-born architect and protégé of the prominent Hudson River estate designer Andrew Jackson Downing. Vaux and Downing, a well-known horticulturist, valued the civilizing effects of green urban spaces. After Downing's accidental death in 1852, Vaux continued the work of his mentor in their Newburgh, NY, office for four years. In 1856 he married and moved to New York City where he established his own successful architecture firm.

As early as 1844, William Cullen Bryant, the famous poet and editor of the *New York Evening Post,* strongly proposed the idea of a public park to save Manhattan Island from excessive commercial development. Vaux was working on the residence of one of the influential commissioners of the future park when he reacted critically to the plans of Chief Engineer Egbert Viele. He convinced the commissioners that such an important civic undertaking needed a better plan and proposed a design competition with a cash prize. The idea was accepted although Viele did contribute two important elements to the design, suggesting transverse roads and the more naturalistic shape of the reservoir rather than a rectangular design.

Frederick Law Olmsted, who was not an architect, was appointed as superintendent under Viele. Although Olmsted is better known, Vaux, the Consulting Architect, is chiefly responsible for the architectural design, the bridges, arches, and the Bethesda Terrace, the heart of Central Park. He collaborated closely with British architect and artist Jacob Wrey Mould. Their work helped to establish what has been called the "Victorian Gothic" style of architecture.

Central Park is a magnet for children with its abundance of activities and facilities that help to make time in the Park enjoyable, edifying and healthful. Here are some places of particular interest to children and their parents or guardians.

Key to locating sites:

W= West Side, E= East Side,
Numbers = Nearest Street

(R) = Restrooms / (F) = Food
(I) = Information

Information kiosks and snack carts can be found throughout the park.

Playgrounds:

Adventure Playground W67
Ancient Playground E84-85 (R)
Robert Bendheim Playground E100 (R)
Bernard Family Playground E108
Pat Hoffman Friedman Playground E79
Heckscher Playground W/C61-63 (R)
Billy Johnson Playground E67
James Michael Levin Playground E77
Mariner's Playground W84-85
Pinetum Swings C85
Playground 72 East E72
Playground 96 East E96
Playground 100 West W100
Playground 110 East E110
Playground 110 West W110
Diana Ross Playground W81
Rudin Family Playground W96-97
Safari Playground W91
Abraham and Joseph Spector
   Playground   W85-86

Tots Playground W68
Wild West Playground W93

Public Facilities; Information, Recreation & Refreshments

The Arsenal (Park Offices)
   at the Zoo E64 (F,R)

Ballfields:

Great Lawn C80-85
Heckscher W/C 63-65 (F)
North Meadow C97-102
Ballplayer's House C65 (F)

Basketball Courts:

   Great Lawn C85
   North Meadow Recreation Center C97

Bicycle Rental C76
Boat Rental E74
   Gondola Ride Boathouse
Bowling and Croquet Greens
   (Lawn Sports Center) W76
Kerbs Boathouse E74 (F, R)
Friedsman Carousel C64-65
Chess and Checker House C64
Children's Zoo E65-66
Delacorte Theater C80 (R)
Fishing Center (Catch and Release) E110
Handball Courts C98
Horse Carriage Rental *(Central Park South)*

Ice Skating Rinks (Seasonal):

   Lasker C107 (F, R)
   Wollman E63 (F, R)

Kerbs Boathouse Café E74 (F, R)
Loeb Boathouse Café E74 (F, R)

*Luce Nature Observatory
(at Belvedere Castle)* C79

Marionette Theater
   at Swedish Cottage W79
Metropolitan Museum of Art E80-84 (F, R)
Mineral Springs (Snack bar) C69 (F, R)
Naumberg Bandshell C71
North Meadow Recreation Center C97 (F, R)
Rumsey Playfield E70-71
   (Site of Summer Stage)
Running Track W&E86-96
Swimming Pool (Lasker) C107 (F, R)
Tavern on the Green W66-67 (F, R)
Tennis Courts W 95-96 (F, R)

Visitors Centers:

Belvedere Castle C79 (I)
The Dairy E65 (I)
Charles A. Dana Discovery Center E110 (I, R)
North Meadow Recreation Center E110 (I, R)
Volleyball Courts C85, C65
   Sand Volleyball Courts C65

Wildlife Conservation Center
   (Central Park Zoo) E63-65 (F, R)
   (212) 439-6518

Of special interest to children:

Alice in Wonderland Statue E75
Balto (Sled Dog) E62
Children's Zoo E65-66
Hans Christian Anderson Statue E74

Safety:

Central Park Information (212) 427-8700
Central Park Police (212) 570-4820

Central Park opens at dawn
   and closes at 1:00 AM

Lost and Found *(unofficial)*
   The Yard W81 (212) 628-1036

W62 facing East from 15th floor